Meet the Steelers

By
Mike Kennedy
with Mark Stewart

NORWOOD HOUSE PRESS

Norwood House Press, P.O. Box 316598, Chicago, Illinois 60631

For information regarding Norwood House Press,
please visit our website at: www.norwoodhousepress.com or call 866-565-2900.

Photo Credits:
  Getty Images (4, 7, 8, 12, 13, 15, 20, 21, 22, 23), Icon SMI (16).
Cover Photos:
  Top Left: Topps, Inc., Top Right: Rafael Suanes/Icon SMI,
  Bottom Left: John Sommers/Icon SMI, Bottom Right: Fleer Corp.
The football memorabilia photographed for this book is part of the authors' collection:
  Page 6) Topps, Inc., Page 10) Joe Greene: Xograph, Inc.; Terry Bradshaw, Franco Harris & Jack Lambert: Topps, Inc.,
  Page 11) Lynn Swann: NFL Pro Set; Rod Woodson & Jerome Bettis: Fleer Corp.; Hines Ward: Topps, Inc.
Special thanks to Topps, Inc.

Editor: Brian Fitzgerald
Designer: Ron Jaffe
Project Management: Black Book Partners, LLC.
Editorial Production: Jessica McCulloch

Library of Congress Cataloging-in-Publication Data
    Kennedy, Mike, 1965-
    Meet the Steelers / by Mike Kennedy with Mark Stewart.
        p. cm. -- (Smart about sports)
    Includes bibliographical references and index.
    Summary: "An introductory look at the Pittsburgh Steelers football team.
    Includes a brief history, facts, photos, records, glossary and fun
    activities"--Provided by publisher.
    ISBN-13: 978-1-59953-397-1 (library edition : alk. paper)
    ISBN-10: 1-59953-397-9 (library edition : alk. paper)
    1. Pittsburgh Steelers (Football team)--History--Juvenile literature. I.
    Stewart, Mark, 1960- II. Title.
    GV956..P57K465 2010
    796.332'640974886--dc22
                                    2010006067

Manufactured in the United States of America in North Mankato, Minnesota.
156N–072010

Contents

Words in **bold type** are defined on page 24.

Coach Bill Cowher leads the cheers during the 2006 season.

The Pittsburgh Steelers

People who live near Pittsburgh, Pennsylvania are tough and hardworking. They expect the same from their football team. That is why they love the Steelers. Like the fans, the team never gives up.

Once Upon a Time

Pittsburgh joined the National Football League (NFL) in 1933. Today, the Steelers are one of the NFL's top teams. They have always put great players on the field.

Ernie Stautner and John Stallworth were two of the best.

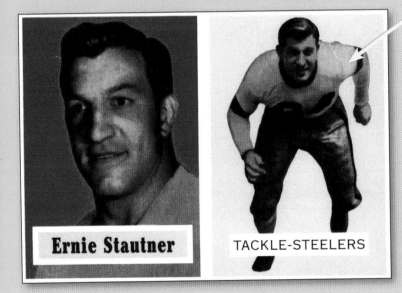

Ernie Stautner

TACKLE-STEELERS

John Stallworth breaks a tackle.

The fans cheer for the Steelers on a chilly day.

At the Stadium

The Steelers play their home games at Heinz Field. It was built in 2001. The wind can be very strong at Heinz Field. This makes it hard to score points. The Steelers don't mind. They play well in bad weather.

Shoe Box

The cards on these pages belong to the authors. They show some of the best Steelers ever.

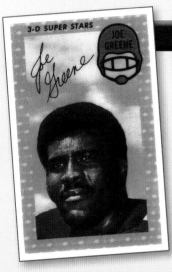

Joe Greene

Defensive Lineman

• 1969–1981

Joe Greene was called "Mean Joe." He was a star of the defense.

Terry Bradshaw

Quarterback

• 1970–1983

Terry Bradshaw led the team to four **Super Bowl** wins.

Jack Lambert

Linebacker

• 1974–1984

Jack Lambert made tackles all over the field.

Franco Harris

Running Back

• 1972–1983

Franco Harris played in the **Pro Bowl** nine times.

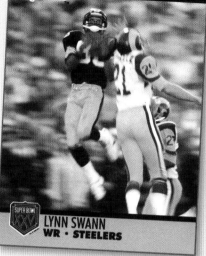

Lynn Swann

Receiver •1974–1982
Lynn Swann jumped high in the air to catch passes.

Rod Woodson

Defensive Back • 1987–1996
Rod Woodson was one of the fastest, smartest Steelers.

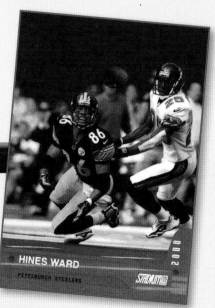

Jerome Bettis

Running Back • 1996–2005
Jerome Bettis was called the "Bus." He was hard to tackle.

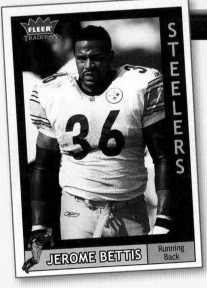

Hines Ward

Receiver • 1998–
Hines Ward could play many positions. He was best at catching passes.

ABC's
of
Football

Look at this picture of Hines Ward (#86). How many things can you find that start with the letter **S**?

See page 23 for answer.

Brain Games

Here is a poem about a famous Steeler:

There once was a Steeler named Troy,
Whose tackles were meant to destroy.
He pounced like a bear,
And had long, flowing hair.
He played every game with great joy.

Guess which one of these facts is **TRUE**:

- *Fans called Troy Polamalu the "Tasmanian Devil."*

- *Troy played running back for the Steelers.*

See page 23 for answer.

Troy Polamalu smiles
after a good play.

The fans cheer for the Steelers.

Fun on the Field

Fans of the Steelers are very loyal. They like to wear black and gold. They sing the team's fight song, "The Pennsylvania Polka." They wave their "Terrible Towels" when the Steelers make a good play.

On the Map

The Steelers call Pittsburgh, Pennsylvania home. The players come from all over the world. These players were named Most Valuable Player (MVP) of the Super Bowl. Match each with the place he was born:

 Franco Harris • **Super Bowl 9 MVP**
Fort Dix, New Jersey

 Lynn Swann • **Super Bowl 10 MVP**
Alcoa, Tennessee

 Terry Bradshaw • **Super Bowl 13 & 14 MVP**
Shreveport, Louisiana

 Hines Ward
• **Super Bowl 40 MVP**
Seoul, South Korea

 Santonio Holmes
• **Super Bowl 43 MVP**
Belle Glade, Florida

United States Map

The Steelers play
in Pittsburgh, Pennsylvania.

World Map

19

What's in the Locker?

The team's home uniform includes a black shirt with gold and white stripes. The team wears gold pants.

LaMarr Woodley wears the team's home uniform.

Pittsburgh's road uniform has a white shirt with gold and black stripes. The team usually wears a black helmet.

James Harrison wears the team's road uniform.

We Won!

From 1975 to 2009, the Steelers won the Super Bowl six times. Super Bowl 43 was a very exciting game. The Steelers scored a **touchdown** with 35 seconds on the clock. They won, 27–23.

The Steelers celebrate their win in Super Bowl 43.

Record Book

These Steelers stars set team records.

Running Back	Record	Year
Franco Harris	14 touchdowns	1976
Barry Foster	1,690 **yards**	1992
Jerome Bettis	111 yards per game	1997

Quarterback/Receiver	Record	Year
Yancey Thigpen	1,398 receiving yards	1997
Hines Ward	112 catches	2002
Ben Roethlisberger	4,328 passing yards	2009

Answer for ABC's of Football

Here are some words in the picture that start with S: Shoe, Sock, Stripe.
Did you find any others?

Answer for Brain Games

The first fact is true. Troy Polamalu got his nickname because he zoomed all over the field. He played defensive back for the team.

Football Words

PRO BOWL
A special game played between the NFL's top stars.

SUPER BOWL
The game that decides the champion of the NFL.

TOUCHDOWN
A scoring play worth six points.

YARDS
A yard is a distance of three feet. A football field is 100 yards from goal line to goal line.

Index

Photos are on **bold** numbered pages.

About the Steelers

Learn more about the Steelers at www.steelers.com

Learn more about football at www.profootballhof.com